Silver

Silver

Rowan Ricardo Phillips

Farrar, Straus and Giroux / New York

Farrar, Straus and Giroux
120 Broadway, New York 10271

Printed in the United States of America
Published in 2024 by Farrar, Straus and Giroux
First paperback edition, 2025

The Library of Congress has cataloged the hardcover edition as follows:
Names: Phillips, Rowan Ricardo, author.
Title: Silver / Rowan Ricardo Phillips.
Description: First edition. | New York : Farrar, Straus and Giroux, 2024.
Identifiers: LCCN 2023038972 | ISBN 9780374611316 (hardback)
Subjects: LCGFT: Poetry.
Classification: LCC PS3616.H467 S55 2024 | DDC 811/.6—dc23/eng/20230926
LC record available at https://lccn.loc.gov/2023038972

Paperback ISBN: 978-0-374-61598-7

Designed by Crisis

Our books may be purchased in bulk for promotional,
educational, or business use. Please contact your local
bookseller or the Macmillan Corporate and Premium
Sales Department at 1-800-221-7945, extension 5442,
or by email at MacmillanSpecialMarkets@macmillan.com.

www.fsgbooks.com
Follow us on social media at @fsgbooks

10 9 8 7 6 5 4 3 2 1

for Núria

Ay, no; no, ay; for I must nothing be.

Therefore no "no," for I resign to thee.

Now, mark me how I will undo myself.

—Richard II

Contents

The First and Final Poem Is the Sun 3

Paradise Lost 4

Rowan Tree 6

Romanticism 7

Atahualpa Yupanqui 9

The Triumph of Song 12

Nobody 14

The Immortal Marsyas 15

El Pintor 16

La Pulga 18

Biographia Literaria 24

A Brief History of Barcelona 25

The Stolen Note 26

Prelude 28

Postlude 31

The Animal Wrestles the Whip from Its Master
and Whips Itself in Order to Become Master 34

Key West 36

Fantasia in a Time of Plague 37

The God of Stories 39

All the Young Dudes 40

Screens 41

Ars Poetica 42

Hole in the Sky 43

Étude No. 5 44

Child of Nature 50

En el tiempo indeciso 57

The First and Final Poem Is the Sun 59

Acknowledgments 61

1, 2, 3, 4 . . .

1, 2 . . .

Silver

The First and Final Poem Is the Sun

Not the meaning but the meaningfulness of this mystery we
    call life
When time, that invention of the mind, finally reveals
What it may have been in the beginning of things and may
    still be in the end
And so scours the Earth in search of what
Is known by a name which is not its true name
And is one thing among billions upon billions of things just
    like it
But aside from the other is the singular essential thing
Which means that poetry is a ritual that the sun organizes
    and arranges
The first and final poem is the sun

Paradise Lost

I start with sorrow,
Then feign joy
In the rhythm method.

I do dark things lightly
And light things darkly.
Opening my front door,

I find the world in flames,
Our tree frozen into rictus
And the front door gone.

But then I listen
For that color, that verb,
That mineral, that metal,

And after, the electric
Data of tattooed angels
Dancing on air.

Hadn't it all
Been something else
Before? Something

Else somewhere
Else to someone
Else before? Could

Be . . . Could be . . .
But the trick,
You see, is to say

That this has never
Been done before,
That it simply sprung up

From some uninhabited
Space: this epic of epics,
This American song.

Rowan Tree

This time I got everything wrong again.
The tree: it was red. And the sky was gray.
Tomorrow ran off with today today.
I'd swallowed time just so I could get things
Right. I was a present to myself but went
Right past it. I called myself it and sat
With it, sad with it, and yet couldn't find
The lie in it. It suited me to a
T. Without it, who would I be? I was
So tired but scared to say it: knowing
What tends to come after—I zipped it.
I parabolaed between parables,
Playing Bach's Concerto in D-Minor,
BWV 974, for
The despair deep in it before
It falls towards the solution
Of its final chord. That's when, in the great
Silver apogee of night, I stepped out
Into the warm air and stripped the rowan
That had been growing there bare until it
Was barely there, roots crowning its nadir,
And everywhere crowing beware beware.

Romanticism

Late autumn in the orange-bronze ranges
And the sky still wet with slaughter, the vote
Done, dying goldenrod tuning the meadows
Beige under flocks of birds that flex the air
Into one black V after another,
Carrying with them the occasional
Silence that flight coaxes from the chest, throat,
And mind, coaxes from altitude's blue view,
Though the bright clear air, no matter how
Clear, is viscous with the virus not dew:
It comes and goes like the heat of the sun,
A heavy haze of grand-scale indifference
To the green commotion of the river,
As I raise my window for one final
Song of summer to leap into my room
And chant to whatever of me is left,
As I shut the window tight and the cold
Burns my nose, as I lean against the glass
For one brief glimpse of God in this world,
What moves in the far-off fade-spectrum
Of the wattage, as daylight grows dimmer
And that feeling that comes and goes, what is it?

I've asked again and again and again
And I so want to tell you it's something
Else, something new, a cure for this world:
So I do and then I don't as I do.

Atahualpa Yupanqui

I

Blue Papa of the cosmic canticles
That the moistened plums sing to throbbing stars,
Stay awhile. It's only morning. The larks
Are still asleep inside your old guitars.
They dream the double dream of free harvests
From a free land far, so far, out of view.
Can you see it? Guitarra, dímelo tú.

II

Once I rode my horse into the center
Of the city and a great silence grew
Deep inside of me—a burning ember
Dwindling down to cinder, but I knew
This silence was not a yes or a no;
And as I'm no poet (there are so few),
Did I dream you? Guitarra, dímelo tú.

III

Come stitch the night back together again,
Don Ata, double god, with your single
String of bass, the one all the quiet pain
Comes easily to, or so it seems in
The wide spectrum of your six silver strings:
Five for what's truthful and one for what's true.
And which am I? Guitarra, dímelo tú.

The Triumph of Song

I mean, the only zone I think I might
Know, and by "know" I mean "this thing hasn't
Quite killed me yet," is the triumph of song.
All my poems mean that, I think, really—

This is the edge of my observable
Universe: I can't see what doesn't sing,
Or what I haven't coaxed from some notes out
Of air. Like the first time I must have heard

"Strawberry Fields Forever." I was twelve
And cupped the soft black sponges to my ears
While sitting cross-legged on a friend's twin bed
As the janky copy of the cassette

Copied over my memory of where
I was, whom I was with, and even who
I was. All I remember is the song,
All that confident lack of confidence,

Which is what writing poems is really like:
The dark blood zoning forwards and backwards
In the brain, the heart like grass in a bowl,
And the burning horizon's sharp swagger

All of it part physics, part faith, part void.

Nobody

I looked for you through a leak in dawn's light
But found you in this cave's mouth dripping spring.
Behind you an orange bubble ripened
In the rain like real flowers in a field
Of memes or a meme in a field of real
Flowers. It is late in the evening
And I forget which huddles for warmth here:
It's not quite time yet or it's damn past time.
Remember what we talked about: Do it.
And then, at daybreak, when the boulder gets
Shoved aside, don't run. Hold on here. And here.
Let life's rugged softness swagger you out.
Life's just that way sometimes: a short sashay
Under a cloud and then a sprint to the sea.

The Immortal Marsyas

O, silver-lyred Apollo

                                        gimme that

El Pintor

By the time you sketch it out they're gone—
A different kind of murder you call art.
It's Thursday and all is ridiculous.
The bourgeoisie, certain that anyone
Else is the bourgeoisie, August-stranded
In the bright ennui of inheritance,
Fall like soldiers onto this coastal town
As a culebrón of clouds, suspended
Minor chords, coax the sun from its sightless
Perch, and pale gold LeBron James jerseys dot
The bars lining the esplanade. *Un bar*
aux Folies Bergère this is not,
And the perspective may or may not be
Messed up, but these people you see only
In the wince of their summer orgasms,
Gouged out from their shells and soft as urchins,
They want in. The back tattoo of the Dutch
Banker, the surgical scar of the Dutch
Banker's wife, the French couples who go Dutch
On breakfast, tapas, dinner, and themselves,

They also want in. Everyone wants in.
To be described, or just some mortal sleep,
That blank canvas behind our closed eyelids
Where dreams save us, and we all become gods.

La Pulga

On a sunny Saturday afternoon in Seville.
On an overcast morning in New York.
Sometime past midnight in Tokyo.
This is how you live now.
This is how you have lived
For nearly half your life.
You're in one place, playing a game,
Which is to say doing your job.
You're in one place and you're in all possible places.
The shorn-smooth grass you walk on—
You mostly walk, like a painter
Wandering a meadow—
Is black ice for the rest of us.
We are infected by data.
We watch you in the simulacrum.
We love you because the simulacrum
Tells us to love you. We hate you because
The simulacrum tells us to hate you.
Some of us have no interest in you at all,
But the simulacrum makes sure

We know who you are.

We all see you. You're standing in one place:

You tend to do this, just take up space someplace and wait.

Your name is stamped between your shoulder blades.

You turn your back on all of us

And it's like your name itself calls for the ball.

And it too knows who you are

As you balance in this field of the lord and focus

Because what you're about to do has no name.

How many years ago was it?

You were an anonymous kid

Sipping an Aquarius in front of the convenience store,

Some spot like a Spar or 7-Eleven called OpenCor.

You were the flea sticking his head out from the passenger's side

Of his cousin's jalopy as it wheezed its way up Carles III.

You were one of the last child prodigies

Before the simulacrum turned prodigies

Into humorless, practiced celebrities.

The last seasons of no internet at home

And a chocolate croissant with the sports papers

And the team training a block up the street.

Day after day, I'd see you on that corner

Slowly sipping the same soft drink day after day,

A kid bored out of his mind, and for that brief

Moment in time,
The proud owner of a street corner in Barcelona.

On a sunny Saturday afternoon in Seville,
On an overcast morning in New York,
Sometime past midnight in Tokyo,
Your teammates seem filed down to the marrow,
Jaded, wading through the long year, dulled
By pains or rust or existential crises,
Men of unfathomable wealth running around
In shorts and feeling the weight of the world
Hovering over them with terrifying delight.
And then you give the ball away.
You give the ball away, which is like giving away
Your mother. You gave the ball away trying something
Mundanely special that didn't work out
And there went the ball, the other team took it,
Ran away with it, and now you're losing.
A minute passes. Another. It's an overcast
Morning in New York. A Saturday afternoon
In Seville. And if you lose nothing really changes.
The reporters will dust off their stories about crisis,
Rub out a malicious rumor or two, ask the same questions
They asked a week ago, everyone in line
Because that's how their food arrives on the table.

More minutes pass. You're losing. You're losing.
Everything is fine, but you're losing.
You're losing and walking and walking. You're losing
And everyone is running by you.
Everyone is running but you. You're not
Even walking now. You just stand there. A vision.

You imagine someone standing to your left,
The length of a blue whale away from you.
There's a ball at his feet. And free to muse
For a moment, he sees you flickering among
A sea of hostile white shirts like the sun parting clouds.
You're surrounded by five sets of pumping arms,
Legs, heaving chests, panic. You simply stand there.
From their lifetimes of amateur mind reading
They think they know what your teammate
Wants to happen. They spy both of you.
They know you. And they think they see you.
You're simply standing there, out on a corner of the action.
But you're invisible to them like a god
And powerful to them like a god; they can feel
The heat when you part the air with a glance.
So they think they know where you are.
They think they see you in the spirit of the grass.
There's a man standing to your left,

The width of a rainbow away from you.
You're standing in negative space now: there are
Three men in front of you, trying to eye you
While spiking themselves into the ground.
There are two more men on either side of you.
Another, in orange, the tallest one of them all,
Stands as wide as he can in the mouth of the goal
Waving his arms like he's trying to scare away a bear.
You're accounted for by all of them.
You're in a place where you can do them no harm.
The only way the ball can arrive to you
Is hours later in a hospital, that prophecy
Of dislocations, broken legs, concussions.
And yet, as all things within the sight of Jupiter
Belong to Jupiter, the ball arrives to you.

When does a habit become a fact? When the ball
Arrives to you. You swing your left foot
Waist-high to meet it. And the ball meets the high corner
Of the goal. The legend of the impossible goal
Is far more plausible, more reasonable than this goal.
You celebrate it as though you now know,
Or suddenly have remembered, that there are no limits
To you. So you do it again, this time with your other foot.
Towards the other high corner of the goal.
Send the ball so softly there it wouldn't break an egg

If one were dangled there. You'd score one more
And assist a fourth. Just another day for you,
Saving another day in your way,
Sending the inner child home happy or distraught
But whether in one state or the other still amazed.
Didn't we talk about this
That day we both decided it was ridiculous
Not to move on from our daily nod,
Like daily bread, and say something instead,
An hola qué tal that I maybe took too far
When I came close to you, the width of a whisper, to tell you
   about the dream I had
That happens light-years in the future
When you score three of the greatest goals
Anyone will ever see, and we all just move on,
As though bored by it all by then, or spoiled,
Like when the greatest love
You'll ever have begins to blend with the paint,
And that feeling, how it won't have been the first time,
And that feeling, how it won't yet be the last time,
Not yet, the last time coming
Some other day in a numb malaise of Burofaxes before the
   tears,
Which is why I felt the need to tell you,
There and then, or here and now,
Before any of it happened, or after it all, that . . .

Biographia Literaria

To write with your reading mind. To read with your writing mind. To be bottomless, atemporal, absent of hierarchy, and just. To keep yourself honest. To keep yourself fictive. To know, deep in your heart, that every poem has already been written. To know that poetry, like the universe itself, began with its smallest particle, the syllable, expanding and contracting through time. To live a little. To die often. To accept that poetry is older than reflex, that it predates intention, that it is the breath your breath takes before you breathe.

A Brief History of Barcelona

Five a.m. in summer: the ABCs
Of summer, and the blue-brown-aubergines
Of a summer dawn before dawn changes
Summer into sea greens, farewells, and gold.
Rain silences the birdsong, but seagulls
Still sweep by as all the city's night-lights
Are snuffed out by silver morning's silver haze.
The imagination hides in plain sight
As the sun's rays in the western night,
Or the soft hustle of those languished stars
That in a sky-blue hex evaporate
From view, never to be seen again, like
A brief history of Barcelona
That begins with "Inshallah" and ends there too.

The Stolen Note

On the most westerly Blasket
In a dry-stone hut
He got this air out of the night.
—Seamus Heaney, "The Given Note"

Ocean-exposed like the smallest Blasket:
Luanda's isthmus, a northernmost hut,
And a sail staring out at it through the night.

They knew that was no crescent moon, had heard
Of others dragged into the white, their tune
Silver as shark and sword and loud weather,

As much a bleak code as a melody.
There was no preparing for it, an ear
Either knew it or not, nothing easy,

A continent turned into an island,
An island turned into pain. Take this thing,
They heard, this is your first violin.

So whether they called it sacred music
Or not, I don't know if I care. Here it
Was: the ancient-modern mid-Atlantic

Song of a somewhere turned into nowhere.
And nowhere to hide they listened gravely,
As an iron note inched closer on air.

Prelude

I

My grandmother saw it coming and left.
I'd already left. It came late and swift
Like a tidal wave mistaken for a wave,
Came, not as a note but as an octave,
Black-keyed and mangled, searching the hospice
Only to find she'd left without notice,
The soul clapped from her body, masked by death,
Death hiding death from death, and finding no
Sign of her in the high cheekbones or skin,
Strode out on a cough into the evening.

II

In the weeks between her death and being
Laid to rest, life became COVID-19.
Both the living and the dead shared one air.
Then the service came, and I was not there.
I watched from the safe distance of an app
As my mother and uncle, masked among
The masked few in a pewless space, made peace
With the orphans who'd come to take their place.
Looking at them on-screen was like looking
Out at the world through the bars of a cage.

III

And now, high on a slope near Van Cortlandt,
The immortelles of perfect pitch sing Ena
Harris to sleep. Her shade goes there to listen
Bathed in the scent of ilex, palm, linden,
Kapok. It is Easter and she is dressed
In her lilac best and hat her daughter
Crossed bridge and Bronx and plague to bring to her.
She is two steps ahead of this pentameter
As it follows her through the flexed valley
Of the shadow of death; this elegy
Which, like all of them, is so useless and late.
My grandmother saw it coming. And she left.

Postlude

Her hospital bed, her favorite red gown,
the one embroidered with small purple
and gold flowers trellising the unknown

infection riddling every inch of her,
her hair brushed back but not braided today,
the lunch tray remaindered to a corner,

plastic pudding cup, nectarine, jaded
pillbox, all hollowed out, verbless, she sang,
didn't sing, and sang, as she cross-faded

to an invisible dimension seen
only on the back of her winced lids,
the flowers sitting on the windowsill,

those photos pinned to the wall, the turquoise
vase, the unused frames, suddenly they seemed
important, where would they all go, I surprised

myself that, for just a second, I'd deemed
those things to be of value in themselves,
all that flared bric-a-brac, and felt ashamed:

I held her hand in search of some resolve
but as her hand trembled my hand trembled,
I was bad at this, I wanted to prove

that I wasn't, my mind reassembled
and, for a moment, shut down; I joined her
where charon sat at a makeshift table

killing time with his dog in the foyer,
playing dominoes by himself, waiting
under the faint spectral light of a coy star;

she was there only in the most craven
sense of the word "there," as when someone says
I'll be there soon when they're still in New Haven,

she squeezed my hand and whistled from the strain,
I rubbed her hand with my free hand, then kissed
it, and then kissed her warm forehead again

as I pried my hand from her grip and missed
my last chance not to have done that, I looked
at the time and saw I had a minute

left, then, after having done all the math,
took a deep breath I can never take back, far
away was a better me who would chant,

she saw it coming so she left, but my car
was waiting downstairs, silver and fine-free,
so I left. The rental purred when I turned

it on, and just like that she was gone.

The Animal Wrestles
the Whip from Its Master
and Whips Itself in Order
to Become Master

In the sheerest light
Of winter, you become the poet
And I become the ringer

In a robin's throat.
I sleep as you sing,
You sleep as I sing,

Finagling the most flagrant
Seasons to forget themselves
In the fragrance of the silver

Fox, the far-off fires dousing the pines.
The right power,
It was the right power,

It was the right power
For the wrong fool.
It was the wrong hour

But the right tool.
A poem of summer surfacing
As a song of force.

A song of force surfacing
As the poem of force.
Beautiful and mutable

But still a thing of force.

Key West

for B.C.

Remembering that little trick of light
In "The Idea of Order at Key West"
When we turn from the singing at the shore,
Shine-minded, ponderous, and raw, to find

There in its debonair, the distant port
Not a mile off now but right here,
High on nocturne and brine, biding its time
In the muddy waters of distortion

That flood Key West till everything
Has happened and nothing that has happened will,
Like the apocryphal songs of yacht rock
Which mean nothing to you until they do.

Fantasia in a Time of Plague

Went to see the River Man
Told him all I could about my plan
He said, "Nah, son . . . I'm good"
You might be surprised
To find that he
Spoke like he was from the hood
But look around
Shade covers every square inch
Of the ground
Night is the political symbol we're unable
To make less literal
A blindness to simple
Basic kindness
That's the hood not the hood
The River Man and all the rivers Milton
Shouted out to for Lycidas understood this
But he was the myth of a mourning kid kidding himself
That he cared about King or sin or killing kings
(But let me take that back—
He got locked up for that)

Poetry is séance and silence and science
Holed up in the hood and haring through the wood
Part pasture and part hood
A rendition of tradition unplanned
Black hoodie pulled back
So the ears can see what the eyes don't see
Like a silver river that bends out of sight
But still roars in your head
As the River Man said it would
On those sleepless nights
When you hear the living
And the dead
Complicit as kites
Rhyming about civil rights.

The God of Stories

I learned to listen to what I see
But never quite to see what I hear
And something has always been missing
In the hearing: unglamorous truth
No that's been there no it's something else:
The origin story of the god
Of stories yes that's it that headless
Moon not swollen with night but the moon
As it dissolves dawn's haptic canvas
That self-portrait of the first silence

All the Young Dudes

He never died and died and lives like that,
Renewed by whatever mewling YouTube
Hot take the hate-hot laptop searing his lap
Calls painful pleasure and then pleasing pain.
Shaken shut, he opened up to the prune
In his head and said he would kill a kid
If he had to, having the aptitude
To do it confirmed by a test he took
A few months prior to changing his look.

Screens

George Floyd's face floats slightly out of focus
The same way a fire always does
Because there is no beginning or end
When you look at either, only the heat,
Remember the heat, how it burns the back
Of the throat as night screams his name through the flames.

Ars Poetica

A poem of the interior
Flooded by the exterior
And lost in Lake Superior
Like the Edmund Fitzgerald or
A bipartisan senator.

Hole in the Sky

His mind kept the airspace but sold the sun.
At night, he ordered his own sun, which was
Supposedly arriving soon, they said,
In entourages of azures and clouds.

A state had been charged with charging him
Then a state was charged for charging him.
The absence of exposition hit home
And so, like a chord that needs resolving

After yeahyeahyeahyeah, he was sent home.
Now things are clear now and so less clear now:
The scent of summer in all autumn sound;
The shore and chatoyance of the sea stones;

And a hayness in the wavelength a black
Horse inhales en route back to the barn. Tune
Me in then tune me out, dead man, with your yeah
Yeah yeah yeah and your big hole in the sky.

Étude No. 5

I

A poem can't begin without its key.
We swam together in the summer slough
As the horizon ushered out the bay,
My dropped fob some crustacean's home by now,
Some blueprint of a place with endless doors
But no entrances or exits, no sign
Blazoned welcome or keep out, so I sing,

II

"We swam together in the summer slough
As the horizon ushered out the bay,
My dropped fob some crustacean's home by now":
A poem can't begin without its key.
Somewhere in that chrome, my mortality,
Somewhere out there, the lives of the poets,
The third geographies, the white egrets.

III

As the horizon ushered out the bay,
My dropped fob some crustacean's home, by now
The poem can't begin. Without a key,
We swam together in the summer slough
Far from the car's hull, its sand-salted bow,
When thirteen silver-ringed sirens emerged
From the distant deep and lit it like a torch.

IV

That late summer in Orient, New York
And all this actually happened. The high flames
Purred to the low, hissing clouds the torque
Of the bay and not the bay itself made
Sulk there and wait for the fires to fade:
Any minute, they said, Any minute.
We'll leave in just a minute. But they didn't.

V

Any minute. Any minute. Any
Minute. Any minute. Any minute.
Any minute. Any minute. Any
Minute. Any minute. Any minute.
Any minute now. Yes. Any minute.
It wasn't the flames it was the sirens.
Night-bold they huddled and opted for violence.

VI

Child of Nature

Five years have past; five summers, with the length
Of five long winters! and again I hear
These waters, rolling from their mountain-springs
—William Wordsworth, "Lines Composed
a Few Miles above Tintern Abbey, On Revisiting
the Banks of the Wye during a Tour. July 13, 1798"

Maybe seven years: or, if not, some length
Of time like that has come and gone. I hear
Them in my head, in the clear mountain-springs
I left behind when I returned again
To my hometown, New York, its steel cliffs
Sag-glassed and star-stunned in the weak impress
Of sunlight and solitude. Years connect
And disconnect me. The winter-sharp sky
And the cold comfort of a cloud in repose
In it that, once seen, vanishes from view
As nature imagines the orchard-tufts
That cloud has passed over, the haloed fruits
The sun and moon steal at dawn for themselves
Before day starts and the talking heads see

Emerging from their foxholes practiced lines
On the sanctity of God and Christ, farms,
The Investor, the glory of coal smoke,
And the movement we need swinging from trees.
Having let be be my center of seem,
I spent a year and a half in the woods
Culling from those cold mountaintops the next fire,
Feeling infinite, and alone.

                    What forms
First: a thing or its form? The I or me?
The maker or the thinker? A bird's-eye
View of the life, what Arnold called the din
Of strife, a little like Floyd's "Us and Them,"
Soothed the doom of numb Zoom rooms. But what sweet
Prison's not still a prison? What kind heart
Isn't bathed in blood? What mind doesn't mind
Being the mind's second act? I was too
Abstract for the Berkshire snowfall, perhaps,
Which day by day flared out like influence
From a concrete dream about abstract life.
The idea being that great nature acts
On all living things in a way we trust,
Or must learn to have faith in; that it is a gift
For the soul of the lingering childmood
In all of us, and makes all mystery

Answerable, all weight bearable weight,
Forty tons of green sighs in a blue world
That wait for an apt word in an apt mood,
Blessed, blue-green, and serene, the mind put on
A pedestal centered in a gold frame
And hung on a sun-warmed wall. But my blood
Circuits the outlines of skylines asleep,
Unwept, and unsung that way—. My soul
Has grown from a Bronx tenement's power.
My Old Testament: a corner store's joy
At being part of the life of things.

                                    This,
As the kids say: facts. Often not oft
Kept me from turning soft, and all the shapes
Of nature turned in on themselves. No stir
Of air was there but for cityworld,
Where nature, in seeing me, cut its heart
Out while singing my country 'tis of thee
And vamped those vaulted buildings into woods,
    Mountains, and streams. My country 'tis of thee.

But now when I think of that lost thought,
Somehow found here in the sudden and faint
Power of sacred songs, perplexity
Sidles in with the setting sun again.

I see the blue sky whiten then brown, sense
John and Paul sharing a spliff and some blurred thoughts
About diminished seventh chords or food
In a small, smoke-soaked hotel room, and hope
One day to finally figure out first
And foremost if this is nature. Roe
On mountains, whistling quail, the burned sides
Of a flowering Rowan tree, green streams
Like on the old maps of the world where man
Painted water olive or jade. No one
Would mistake any of these, now or then,
For something unnatural. There were days
When I was a child when I would walk by
Storefronts tattooed with graffiti, the paint
Still fresh from the can, the tart cataract
Of aerosols clouding the mind, a rock
Through the veined window, a pale mash of wood
From a smashed guitar splintered like hay, "Me
So Horny" oozing from some boombox love
Stowed away from sight, and a lucky charm
Left on the doorknob and of interest
To no one but Tanya, who'd just walked past,
Stopped, turned back, took it, and said, Got one more
For my collection, yeah boy! What was this
If not one of nature's many strange gifts?
Or, is nature only what you believe

When you read? The hill-and-dale flex I learned?

The "Fern Hill" flex I learned alone and, hour

After hour, finding it oftentimes

Pure musical reflex, humanity

Responding in song to the strange power

Of an environment enhanced and felt,

Finally, instead of simply seen, joy

Inching along the cracks of the sublime,

Like the music of a glass interfused

With the life of all people, all stars, suns,

And the sounds of it all shattering air

Before the glass itself shatters. Oh man,

I grew tired of whatever impels

Nature to always be elsewhere, and thought:

Listen, yes, I have trees and rivers still,

Yes, I have gardens and ponds, I have woods,

I have a romantic park that was (behold!)

Once Seneca Village razed from the world.

I've had these things and what they half create,

Which is just half of what I recognize

And welcome as nature in its own sense.

For all park is policy, all verse is nurse,

Every habitat a cradle for the soul.

At least for the time being.

Or perchance

There are words, like "perchance," that function more
Or less like what I meant to say, decay
Being part of the process, faint cloud-banks
Frothing then finished by the wind, part-friend
Part-foe of what the mind sets out to catch
Whenever and wherever it can, read
Or listened to under sun or streetlights.
I too crave a bright ocean meadow while
The sun braids the green with its warm gold. Once,
This seemed the only way to be and make
A natural world. But I can't betray
Where I'm from. I don't want that privilege.
That doesn't mean neighborhoods sprayed in lead
Are like emerald meadows that inform
And reassure naturally, impress
Love onto the heart naturally, feed
Naturally on nature's summer-tinged tongues
Of chartreuse verbs gifted to the human,
But what exists between them is both all
There is and nothing at all, like life
Grown out of the fiction of poems. Disturb
What cannot be disturbed, and then behold
As it awakens and sings to the moon

In the late morning haze. This is the walk,
The long walk, from which I have emerged free
At last, after a journey of light-years
Across a field of dead ideas matured
To life for their own sake, free in my mind,
Finally, to remember all the forms
Of my life enhanced by this dwelling-place,
Its hard-edged abracadabra, heathen
Sunday mornings, and phosphorescent grief.
No one is ever alone with their thoughts.
Alone on a cliff or here beside me,
We are crowded by presence and perchance
Where listening to stream and street we hear
The other, even as one of them gleams,
And the other gleams we can't forget
One or the other: ethereal stream
And electric street are parts of the same long
Link in the same human chain—. I came
To this poem, the long one, with a lot to say.
I'd sung my art before this with real zeal,
Chanting through three moods so as not to forget:
The ground, then heaven, then the weapon. Years
Passed. And now from my high window, the cliffs
And canyons of these avenues call me
Back to sing through fire for their sweet sake.

En el tiempo indeciso

The horizon hour with its awful
Power puts all abandoned dreams to bed.

Stars. Stars gone. Glaucous clucksong. Dawn. Sky. Sky
And the vanishing of tomorrow's plane

As it describes the future in its fade:
The plane silver, its vapor trail silver,

Silver filling the spaces where they've been.
And I—no, no I; you will see for yourself

And I will be nothing but poetry,
A blank in the blankness of the long game,

I as ambiguous as algebra,
Something cosmic mistaken for something

Chronic, some flex to figure out as it
Blows the heart open approaching the end

Of the self, the one you bought the ticket for,
That temporary solution for X.

The First and Final Poem Is the Sun

The first and final poem is the sun
Which means that poetry is a ritual that the sun organizes
    and arranges
But aside from the other is the singular essential thing
And is one thing among billions upon billions of things just
    like it
Is known by a name which is not its true name
And so scours the Earth in search of
What it may have been in the beginning of things and may
    still be in the end
When time, that invention of the mind, finally reveals
Not the meaning but the meaningfulness of this mystery we
    call life

Acknowledgments

Acknowledgments are due to the editors of the following magazines, in which some of these poems—at times in earlier versions—have appeared: AGNI, Broadcast, The Cortland Review, The New York Review of Books, The New Yorker, The Night Heron Barks, The Paris Review, Peripheries, Ploughshares, Poetry, Poetry London, The Poetry Review, Smartish Pace, The Threepenny Review, The Times Literary Supplement, and The Yale Review. "Fantasia in a Time of Plague" first appeared in Together in a Sudden Strangeness: America's Poets Respond to the Pandemic, edited by Alice Quinn (New York: Alfred A. Knopf, 2020). "Nobody" first appeared in a limited-edition printing for Princeton University's 2021 Phi Beta Kappa induction ceremony.